WILDERNESS

THE ESSENTIAL GUIDE TO HARD TIMES

REVISED EDITION

by

Wm. W. Wells

Independently published: William W. Wells. Bacliff, Texas.

ISBN: 9798396956131

TABLE OF CONTENTS

6. David in the Wilderness

CHAPTER 1: INTRODUCTION

> Then Samuel said to Jesse, "Are all your sons here?" And he said, "There remains yet the youngest, but behold, he is keeping the sheep." And Samuel said to Jesse, "Send and get him, for we will not sit down till he comes here." (1st Sam. 16:11).

How This Book Came About

Several years ago, I taught a series on the life of David for the youth at my church. The concept was to match the history of David, as found in First and Second Samuel, with relevant Psalms of David. In particular, I was interested in the Psalms which the Septuagint, (the first Greek translation of the Hebrew Bible), attached to specific historical moments in the life of David.

The series was meant to encourage open discussions with the youth in my class. The concept was to look at some of the salient points in the life of David, and to try to pry open what was going on in David's thoughts and feelings through a look at relevant Psalms. For this reason, I have included discussion questions at the end of each chapter. If you are using this book for personal study, use those questions to think more deeply about the thoughts and feelings that these events may stir up.

Pay special attention to how David is developing the leadership skills that will one day make him a great king.

Since there are very few psalms attached to specific events in David's life after his wilderness experience, it made sense to limit the discussion to his life and times up until David is first crowned king. The result is a deep dive into some of the more trying times in the life of Israel's future king.

This revised edition is intended to make the book easier to use for Bible studies, with the inclusion of readings for each chapter. I have broken apart some chapters in order to make for shorter Bible readings. There is also an added chapter on the close relationship between David and Jonathan.

Anointing a Future King

Reading: 1st Samuel 16:1 to 17:19

Our first introduction to the future king is when the prophet Samuel is instructed by God, "Fill your horn with oil, and go. I will send you to Jesse the Bethlehemite, for I have provided for myself a king among his sons" (1st Sam. 16:1). Samuel is reluctant owing to the fact that Saul, the current king, whom he had anointed previously, is not likely to look kindly on Samuel anointing a new king (1st Sam. 16:1-2). God tells him to disguise the act as a simple sacrifice to the Lord.

> Samuel did what the LORD commanded and came to Bethlehem. The elders of the city came to meet him trembling and said, "Do you come peaceably?" And he said, "Peaceably; I have come to sacrifice to the LORD. Consecrate yourselves, and come

> with me to the sacrifice." And he consecrated Jesse and his sons and invited them to the sacrifice (1st Sam. 16:4-5).

Why are the elders trembling? They know that there is tension between Samuel and King Saul. Their last meeting ended with Samuel telling Saul, "The LORD has torn the kingdom of Israel from you this day and has given it to a neighbor of yours, who is better than you" (1st Sam. 15:28). The prophet tries to reassure them that he is not there to cause trouble, he is just there to sacrifice. His real purpose is to anoint a future king, but this is a secret mission. Such an action would be seen as a declaration of rebellion, so the matter is meant to stay private until God's timing is full.

When the great prophet arrives at the feast, Eliab, Jesse's eldest son, is presented before him. Samuel thinks, "Surely the LORD's anointed is before him" (1st Sam. 16:6). The current king Saul, whom Samuel had anointed originally, was very tall (1st Sam. 10:23). Here again was a tall and handsome warrior, surely, this young man would make an excellent king. But, God said, "Do not look on his appearance or on the height of his stature, because I have rejected him. For the LORD sees not as man sees: man looks on the outward appearance, but the LORD looks on the heart" (1st Sam. 16:7).

One by one, Jesse parades each of his seven favorite sons before Samuel. One by one, God says no (1st Sam. 16:8-10). Seven sons are presented, but not one is chosen by God. Samuel is sure that he is hearing from God, so what is wrong?

Young David

Not intending to present David, Jesse, David's father, has not even called David to be present at this feast. It is likely that David knows very little of what is happening. Samuel is not interested in Jesse's thoughts on the matter, he is only interested in God's thoughts on the matter.

> Then Samuel said to Jesse, "Are all your sons here?" And he said, "There remains yet the youngest, but behold, he is keeping the sheep." And Samuel said to Jesse, "Send and get him, for we will not sit down till he comes here" (1st Sam. 16:11).

We know of David as the great king of Israel. But this young boy David was not getting the vote as most likely to succeed. We don't know many details, but we do know that he was constantly tending the sheep, while there is never a mention of his brothers doing the same. When the brothers go to war, David is sent to bring them supplies. It would appear that he was treated more like a servant than a son. Was there some reason why he was singled out in this way? We don't know. What we do know is that when Samuel arrives to anoint a new king, Jesse only calls his seven older sons, but not David.

When David appears, the first thing that Samuel notices is that he was ruddy (1st Sam. 16:12). This young man surely spent most of his time out of doors. The prophet looks on this bright-eyed young man, and God tells him, "Arise, anoint him, for this is he" (1st Sam. 16:12).

Samuel anoints David, and the Spirit of the LORD rushes upon the boy (1st Sam. 16:13). Now you would think that David's stock would have risen sharply in the family circle, but keep reading—Saul needs psalmists, musicians skillful at soothing him when he is agitated. David's name is mentioned and so he is sent for. Where is he? David is still with the sheep (1st Sam. 16:19).

Maybe David was just there training a replacement. Well, turn to the next chapter. The Philistines have gathered for war. Standing as the champion of the Philistine army is a giant of a man. The Israelite army is terrified of this Goliath. David's three oldest brother's Eliab, Abinadab, and Shammah have been sent to join Saul's army (1st Sam. 17:13). David, who now serves Saul as a psalmist, also continues to go back and forth to Bethlehem to feed his father's sheep (1st Sam. 17:15). It was common for those who served the king to serve for several months and then return home for the remainder of the year. After all that has happened to honor David, when he returns home, his family is still treating him like a servant.

So comes the day that Jesse sends David on an errand: "Take for your brothers an ephah of this parched grain, and these ten loaves, and carry them quickly to the camp to your brothers. Also take these ten cheeses to the commander of their thousand. See if your brothers are well, and bring some token from them." (1st Sam. 17:17-18).

Notice that there are still four other brothers available to send, but David is the one who is sent to carry supplies to his elder brothers. His father has to explain to David what is occurring. It appears that David has been left so far out of the loop concerning family matters that Jesse has to tell David that three of his older brothers have left to join Saul's army.

There seems to be a huge disconnect between God's valuation of David and how he valued by his family and likely the family friends and neighbors. We assume that David's skill as a shepherd was well known. The other thing that we do know is that young David had an impressive reputation as someone who could sing and play the harp. He was not only a great musician, but he wrote his own psalms. It was likely that he had become a great psalmist on all those lonely nights tending sheep. In any case, he was now one of those who served king Saul personally, singing and playing his harp. This should have raised his reputation in the neighborhood.

Discussion Points:

1. What was David's value in the eyes of his family? What might the reasons for this be? How do you suppose this affected his value in the eyes of his friends and neighbors?

2. How do you suppose this affected David's own self-evaluation?

3. Why do you suppose that God chooses David, above his brothers?

4. It says that the Spirit of the Lord rushed upon David (1st Sam. 16:13). What do you suppose that looked like? Do you think that his father and his brothers noticed?

Application:

1. It appears that David's family did not value him very highly, even as he was being honored and respected by others. How do you think your family sees you? How do you suppose the attitude of your family affects your value in the eyes of other friends and neighbors?

2. We know that David appears confident in his skills. And we do know that his skill with the psalms was recognized. But we don't have a clear picture of how young David saw himself? Did his self-esteem suffer from his low regard in the family? How do you see yourself? Does your own self-esteem affect how others see you?

3. David is chosen for a special place in God's kingdom. What do you think God sees in you? Do you think God has a special place for you in His kingdom? When you look at the people around you, do you think God has a special purpose for them?

4. It says that when Samuel anointed David, and the Spirit of God rushed upon him. Have you experienced the Spirit of God touching you in a personal way? What do you experience in these moments? Are there specific ways that your body reacts? How do your thoughts and emotions react?

16. David in the Wilderness

CHAPTER 2: THE GIANT SLAYER

> And David said to the men who stood by him, "What shall be done for the man who kills this Philistine and takes away the reproach from Israel? For who is this uncircumcised Philistine, that he should defy the armies of the living God?" (1st Sam. 17:26).

The Anointing Activates

Reading: 1st Samuel 17:22-58

When David arrives at the front lines searching for his brothers, Goliath appears, sneering at the troops of Israel, while they fled from him, cowering at his stature. "Have you seen this man who has come up?" David is listening to the men exclaim, "the king will enrich the man who kills him with great riches and will give him his daughter and make his father's house free in Israel" (1st Sam. 17:25).

Not at all intimidated by Goliath, David's interest is peeked, "What shall be done for the man who kills this Philistine and takes away the reproach from Israel? For who is this uncircumcised Philistine, that he should defy the armies of the living God" (1st Sam. 17:26)? David begins in the way of the world, the way of the conversation in front of him, "What shall be done for the man…?" There are riches and honor to be gained.

Although, David's vision starts self-focused, his thoughts shift immediately. He envisions the man who "takes away the reproach from Israel," and finally indignantly asks, "who is this uncircumcised Philistine, that he should defy the armies of the living God" (1st Sam. 17:26)? The anointing on David is enlarging David's heart. He no longer sees himself as a shepherd of sheep, even though his family still sees him in that role, he is now, without any worldly title or direction, the shepherd of Israel. This is the destiny spoken over him when Samuel poured the oil of anointing over him. Looking down on this defiant Philistine before whom all of Israel cowered, it would seem that David's heart "grew two sizes that day."

David's brother hasn't any idea of what is happening:

> Now Eliab his eldest brother heard when he spoke to the men. And Eliab's anger was kindled against David, and he said, "Why have you come down? And with whom have you left those few sheep in the wilderness? I know your presumption and the evil of your heart, for you have come down to see the battle" (1st Sam. 17:28).

Present when Samuel anointed David, the event has had no impact on Eliab. He is accusing David of playing hooky from his job tending sheep. It is clear that Eliab, and we have to assume the rest of the family, has a low opinion of David.

Eliab, like the rest of the troops of Israel, sees the giant Philistine as a river too big to cross. David sees a giant who is insulting God's people, in front of God. David is embracing

God's people because God asked him to. I sincerely doubt that any of this is coming out of David because of some conscious deliberation on his part. His destiny is being released, so his heart's cry has changed. It just bubbles up like a fresh spring. This spring has the fragrance of heaven in it.

The sneer takes David off guard, "What have I done now? Was it not but a word" (1st Sam. 17:29)? The situation before David, the situation before Israel, the situation before God, has pushed all of the normal family dynamics so far away that David seems to struggle to understand Eliab's taunt.

By some miracle of heaven, this young man is sent on behalf of the armies of Israel, not dressed for war, but dressed as a shepherd, staff in hand, with a pouch full of stones and a sling (1st Sam. 17:40). The Israelites are undoubtedly wondering what is wrong with Saul's thinking, allowing David to step out on behalf of all Israel dressed as a shepherd. Saul is probably thinking the same thing. Goliath is fuming at the insult. Confident that he is there with God beside him, David approaches the angry man declaring,

> "You come to me with a sword and with a spear and with a javelin, but I come to you in the name of the LORD of hosts, the God of the armies of Israel, whom you have defied. This day the LORD will deliver you into my hand, and I will strike you down and cut off your head. And I will give the dead bodies of the host of the Philistines this day to the birds of the air and to the wild beasts of the earth, that all the earth may know that there is a God in Israel, and that all this assembly may know that the

> LORD saves not with sword and spear. For the battle is the LORD's, and he will give you into our hand" (1st Sam. 17:45-47).

David is speaking with boldness, and with indignation at the insult cast upon God's chosen people. He has absolute confidence in God's intention to defeat the Philistine threat. Why is David, in his boldness, so much fiercer than all of the rest of Israel's army? Why this concern for the dignity of Israel? How does he know that the battle is the Lord's? It is all in the anointing. It is all in the prophetic words spoken over him, fixing his destiny. David has seized the word, felt its impact, believed the word, and is now taking his first step into the words pronounced by Samuel.

A New Man

We know the story, David rushes forward and strikes the Philistine down with a sling stone. In case you are wondering, a stone thrown from a sling can travel at up to one-hundred miles per hour. It is a deadly weapon. David then proceeds to take Goliath's own sword and behead him. The Philistine army is thunderstruck and loses all courage. As the Philistines turn to run, the army of Israel suddenly rises up with fresh courage and descends upon the terrified Philistines. The army of Israel wins a great victory this day.

David is no longer a shepherd boy; he has become a leader of men. I imagine that this situation is similar to that of the person with a well thought out plan that can quickly control a meeting. So too, a person whose destiny is matched to them can quickly begin to see the vision and become the embodiment of that destiny. The vision that God has planted in David's heart has turned him into a person who influences all those around him. This forgotten shepherd boy has become the most significant leader in the history of Israel, outside of Moses. God, through the prophet Samuel, has matched heaven's desire with the young man David. He is well prepared to begin. He has spent countless hours braving the weather, wild animals and loneliness. He has spent countless hours talking to God, worshiping God, and learning the heart of heaven. David is ready for phase two of his training.

It is important to remember that this destiny is from heaven. David doesn't see it, Samuel doesn't see it, David's family definitely doesn't see it, but God sees it. God saw it in Saul, but Saul failed to step into the role heaven intended for him. God's trust in David has given him the push. Now David is stepping into the vision; the heart of heaven is being released with every step. It will be fifteen years before he becomes king of the southern kingdom Judah. But already David sees the world differently and acts differently. Like a fine steel blade, he will find himself heated, hammered and suddenly cooled many times before he becomes the king after God's own heart.

Discussion Points:

1. What do you think might have contributed to David's preparation to receive God's anointing?

2. God has chosen David and matched him to heaven's desire. How does this change David's life?

3. Destiny is re-direction, not an accomplishment. How do we see this in David's life, even when he doesn't appear to be anywhere close to his life to come?

Application:

1. The anointing that David has on his life gives him an indignation and a boldness in facing Goliath. Has your relationship with God changed you? Do you see things differently now? Do you react differently to situations that you encounter?

2. In retrospect, we can see how many of the things in David's life were preparing him for his role as king. We can also see that the way that David's reactions to his circumstances increases his ability to wear the mantle of God's anointed king of Israel well. Does God have a special desire for you? Are you cultivating heaven's destiny for your life?

3. Destiny is re-direction, not an accomplishment. David steps into his God-given role by his attitudes and courage in standing for the heart of God. What sort of destiny do you think that God has for you personally? How might that change your attitudes and behaviors?

24. David in the Wilderness

CHAPTER 3: ISRAEL'S SUPER-STAR

And the women sang to one another as they celebrated, "Saul has struck down his thousands, and David his ten thousands" (1st Sam. 18:7).

David's Self-Worth

Reading: 1st Samuel 18 & 19

With the head of Goliath in his hand, David is no longer ignored. Saul takes him into his service and no longer allows him to return home (1st Sam. 18:2). Jonathan, the son of Saul, and therefore next in line to be king, befriends David. Their friendship becomes close and the two make a covenant with each other. David goes out to battle clothed in Jonathan's own armor (1st Sam. 18:3-4) as a sign of their mutual respect. Successful at everything Saul sends him to do, Saul makes David a general over his armies (1st Sam. 18:5). David is greatly beloved by the people as well (1st Sam. 18:7). Possibly for the first time in his life, David is admired and respected publicly; he is in an important position and he is excelling.

David is extremely loyal to Saul, even when Saul is trying to kill him, which is about to happen. Perhaps he saw Saul's initial respect for him as the respect of a father, since it appears that his own father was a poor representative of fatherhood, at least to him. David has become a very close friend of Jonathan, Saul's son, so it is possible that he felt that he now had a real family.

Part of the promise to the man who slays Goliath was the hand of Saul's daughter in marriage (1st Sam. 17:25). Saul suggests that David marry Merab his oldest daughter, but David balks, saying, "Who am I, and who are my relatives, my father's clan in Israel, that I should be son-in-law to the king" (1st Sam. 18:18)? It is worth noting that this is at a time when David's reputation is becoming such that Saul is becoming jealous of David. Saul is secretly hoping to entice David into recklessness that will get him killed.

Changing his mind, Saul marries Merab off to another man (1st Sam. 18:19). Later Saul will have his servants suggest David marry Michal, Saul's younger daughter. Again, David replies, "Does it seem to you a little thing to become the king's son-in-law, since I am a poor man and have no reputation" (1st Sam. 18:23)? Despite the fact that David is highly esteemed in Israel, to the point that King Saul himself is dangerously jealous of him, David sees himself as a poor and lightly esteemed man; his own self-image hasn't caught up with the man that he has become.

David in Saul's Kingdom

As Saul and David are returning from a successful campaign against the Philistines, the women come out to greet them. They sing and dance with joy singing, "Saul has slain his thousands, and David his ten thousands." (1st Sam. 18:7). Unfortunately, Saul was a very self-conscious king. Moreover, he lived in a time when palace coups were common. He feared David and was jealous of David's reputation. The Bible tells us:

> And Saul was very angry, and this saying displeased him. He said, "They have ascribed to David ten thousands, and to me they have ascribed thousands, and what more can he have but the kingdom?" And Saul eyed David from that day on.
>
> The next day a harmful spirit from God rushed upon Saul, and he raved within his house while David was playing the lyre, as he did day by day. Saul had his spear in his hand. And Saul hurled the spear, for he thought, "I will pin David to the wall." But David evaded him twice.
>
> Saul was afraid of David because the LORD was with him but had departed from Saul (1st Sam. 18:8-12).

In a moment, through no fault of his own, David goes from being the king's favorite to being the king's most dangerous opponent. On David's part, it must have seemed like a return to a familiar pattern of rejection within the "family," although Jonathan, and, we will see that soon, Michal, Saul's daughter, love him. David respects Saul and does his best to show it, but it is of no use.

Saul in Comparison

It should be remembered that Samuel had originally anointed Saul to be the king of Israel, but that when it came time to crown him king, Saul could not be found (1st Sam. 10:20-24).

The Lord shows Samuel that Saul was hiding in the luggage. It seems that Saul begins with low self-esteem. While I don't know that I would accuse David of low self-esteem, he surely doesn't exhibit high self-esteem. His self-image has definitely not transformed into self-importance.

Unlike David, Saul changes rapidly once he becomes king. After a successful military campaign against the Ammonites, Saul's poorly armed and poorly manned army is facing a very large and well-armed Philistine army (1st Sam. 13:1-7). His army is waiting for Samuel to come and sacrifice for their success. Saul becomes impatient and decides to make the sacrifice himself (1st Sam. 13:9). So now, Saul has, in his mind, added High Priest to his list of titles.

Samuel comes to inform Saul,

> "You have done foolishly. You have not kept the command of the LORD your God, with which he commanded you. For then the LORD would have established your kingdom over Israel forever. But now your kingdom shall not continue. The LORD has sought out a man after his own heart, and the LORD has commanded him to be prince over his people, because you have not kept what the LORD commanded you" (1st Sam. 13:13-14).

No lesson has been learned. Saul continues to do things his own way until Samuel must inform him that he has been rejected by the Lord (1st Sam. 15:26-28).

Dodging Spears

To return to David's story, it is clear that the anointing that was on Saul, is now on David. Unfortunately for Saul, everyone loves David. He was a very successful military leader. Whatever he did, he seemed to prosper. If Saul is going to regain the upper hand and get rid of David, he has to be cunning.

Saul's younger daughter Michal loves David. Thinking that he can induce David into reckless battle with the Philistines and, thus, get him killed, Saul promises Michal's hand in marriage for a dowry of one-hundred foreskins of the Philistines (1st Sam. 18:20-25). Warrior that he is, David rises to the challenge and brings 200 foreskins to Saul, so Saul has no choice but allow David to marry Michal (1st Sam. 18:27).

Saul is distraught. His son Jonathan loves David. Michal, his daughter, is happily married to David. His whole kingdom seems to love David, all while "an evil spirit from God" is plaguing him with a murderous spirit of jealousy.

Saul calls for the murder of David (1st Sam. 19:1), so David must make an escape, with Michal's help. David doesn't have any idea of where to go, so he goes to the place that seems the most sensible, to Samuel. Saul sends men to chase David down. Three squadrons come under the power of the Spirit in Samuel's presence. They begin to prophecy until Saul himself comes and he too goes under the power of the Spirit as well (1st Sam. 19:18-24).

Discussion Points:

1. What similarities might we see between Saul, before he is anointed, and David, before his anointing, that made them ripe for their respective anointing? How might they have been different before their anointing?

2. Think about King Saul for a moment. He, too, had the anointing of God on his life. What happened that caused that anointing to shift from Saul to David?

3. Comparing Saul's reaction to fame and fortune, with that of David, can you see the beginnings of what makes David a "man after God's heart?"

4. Besides being a successful military general, what do you suppose made David so beloved by everyone?

Application:

1. While Saul fails to embrace his destiny, David proves worthy of the anointing on him. Do you feel you have a God-given destiny? What in your life might be preparing you for that destiny?

2. While success goes to Saul's head immediately, it doesn't seem to alter David's character in the same way. How do you handle success?

3. The original rock-star, David was beloved by almost everyone. Still, he seems to think of himself as less than a rock-star. How do you see yourself? How does that compare with how others see you?

32. David in the Wilderness

CHAPTER 4: DAVID AND JONATHAN

> Then Jonathan said to David, "Go in peace, because we have sworn both of us in the name of the LORD, saying, 'The LORD shall be between me and you, and between my offspring and your offspring, forever'" (1st Sam. 20:42).

The Covenant

Reading: 1st Samuel 20

David is having a hard time believing that Saul really wants to kill him, so he goes back to his true friend Jonathan, "What have I done? What is my guilt? And what is my sin before your father, that he seeks my life" (1st Sam. 20:1)?

The two devise an elaborate plan to test Saul's intentions, and to transmit the verdict to David who is to remain hidden from Saul's guards. But, before parting, they strengthen their covenant: "And Jonathan made a covenant with the house of David, saying, 'May the LORD take vengeance on David's enemies'" (1st Sam. 20:16). It is a curious oath, as David's enemy of the moment seems to be Jonathan's own father.

When Jonathan sits down to a meal with his father, it quickly becomes clear that Saul has every intention of murdering David. A protesting Jonathan is then assailed by is father:

> Then Saul's anger was kindled against Jonathan, and he said to him, "You son of a perverse, rebellious woman, do I not know that you have chosen the son of Jesse to your own shame, and to the shame of your mother's nakedness? For as long as the son of Jesse lives on the earth, neither you nor your kingdom shall be established. Therefore send and bring him to me, for he shall surely die" (1st Sam. 20:30-31).

When Jonathan protests further, Saul sends a spear hurling his way. And so, the matter is settled. Jonathan goes to let David know the bad news; he must flee to save his life. Before David departs, the two renew their "covenant of the LORD" (1st Sam. 20:8):

> Then Jonathan said to David, "Go in peace, because we have sworn both of us in the name of the LORD, saying, 'The LORD shall be between me and you, and between my offspring and your offspring, forever.'" And he rose and departed, and Jonathan went into the city (1st Sam. 20:42).

A Remarkable Friendship

There are some important things to notice about the friendship of these two young men. First, Jonathan is the king's son and heir apparent to the throne. He is loyal to his father, but he is also loyal to David, which places him in an awkward position. He is constantly defending David to his father, by which he is able to cool his father's bad temper for a time. In the end, however, his further attempts to defend David only to incur his father's wrath.

David is a newcomer to the halls of power politics, while Jonathan sits at the right hand of the king. Jonathan was likely older than David by about ten years. Thus, his deference to David is unexpected. He seems to see in David something that David himself does not see, his anointing and his destiny.

Against this backdrop, David treats both Saul and Jonathan with the deference their respective offices expect. Despite his familiarity and friendship with Jonathan, David always remains respectful. When it is clear that he must flee from Saul, "David rose from beside the stone heap and fell on his face to the ground and bowed three times" (1st Sam. 20:41). We will see than in subsequent chapters, David remains respectful of Saul, even while he is being hunted by him. He continually blames Saul's judgments against him, not on Saul himself, but on the evil counsel of those around him.

The fact that circumstances were forcing them apart, meant that David's life was now in danger and Jonathan was losing a friend whom he could trust to defend his interests at all cost. This parting opened both men to dangers and personal loss. "And they kissed one another and wept with one another, David weeping the most" (1st Sam. 20:41).

One Last Meeting

There is one more meeting between the two men. David is on the run, with Saul's army attempting to track him down to kill him, when Jonathan comes to David. It is curious that Jonathan is able to locate David while his father's army is chasing hither and yon looking for the fugitive. The most interesting thing to note in this meeting is that Jonathan believes that David will be the next king of Israel, even while Jonathan is the heir apparent.

> And Jonathan, Saul's son, rose and went to David at Horesh, and strengthened his hand in God. And he said to him, "Do not fear, for the hand of Saul my father shall not find you. You shall be king over Israel, and I shall be next to you. Saul my father also knows this." And the two of them made a covenant before the LORD. David remained at Horesh, and Jonathan went home (1st Sam. 23:16-18).

Perhaps, even more telling in this encounter is that Jonathan believes that his father Saul also believes that David will be the next king of Israel. David's leadership skills and military prowess has secured his place in the hearts of all of Israel, even while he is being pursued as a rebel and a traitor. His ability is such that Jonathan expresses that he would be happy to see David be the next king, while he serves at his side.

Discussion Points:

1. David appears to be a rival to Jonathan's power and authority. Why does Jonathan love him so much?

2. Saul has attempted to kill David with a spear on more than one occasion. Why does David continue to serve him faithfully?

3. David has gone from one set of odd family dynamics to another. What strengths or weaknesses might he have learned that help him in his relations with Saul and Jonathan?

4. We know that David has been anointed to be king. Does David seem to be conscious of this as his destiny? Since the anointing was done in secret, why are others so conscious of his destiny?

Application:

1. David appears to be a rival to Jonathan's power and authority. How do you react to rivals to your position, say in the workplace, or on the sports field?

2. We see that David preferred to think well of people, even when they behaved badly. How do you think of people generally?

3. David's family life appears to have been dysfunctional, but he seems to use his experiences well. How does your own upbringing impact your present circumstances for better or for worse? Are you able to use bad experiences for the better?

4. It seems that everyone around David could see his God-given destiny. Do you know what your God-given destiny is? Are there others who seem to know your destiny better than you do?

CHAPTER 5: NOB & GATH

> So he changed his behavior before them and pretended to be insane in their hands and made marks on the doors of the gate and let his spittle run down his beard (1st Sam. 21:13).

The Escape

Reading: 1st Samuel 21
Psalms 34, 52 & 56

David escapes to Nob where there is a large community of priests (1st Sam. 21:1). When things go badly, David looks for the men of God. His last escape was to Samuel, but that put Samuel in danger. He knows that he can't stay long in Nob for fear of putting the community in danger.

When David arrives, Ahimelech the priest of Nob is nervous. He has heard rumors, but David assures him that all is well. David has fled with a small group of men without having the opportunity to return home for supplies.

Ahimelech doesn't have much on hand. He has the day-old bread of the presence, the holy bread placed on the alter daily. This bread is normally only meant for the priests and Levites. It is offered to David and his men who gratefully accept. In addition, David asks for a weapon, as he has had to flee without one. As it is, Goliath's sword, which David took from the giant after he slew him, has been kept there. Accepting the sword, David departs with his men.

Unfortunately, they have been seen by an Edomite, in the king's service, by the name of Doeg who will inform Saul of this visit. This will cause a problem which David doesn't see as yet. It doesn't occur to David that anyone would kill priests.

David slips into Philistine territory. It makes sense that if he hides out in Gath, a large Philistine city state, no will know him, and Israelites are unlikely to travel to Philistine territory, Saul most particularly. Unfortunately for David, one of the servants of Achish, the king of Gath, recognizes him. The servants call David the "king of the land" and know well the song of the women of Israel "Saul has struck down his thousands, and David his ten thousands" (1st Sam. 21:11). It seems that David has leapt from the frying pan into the fire. Thinking quickly, he feigns madness (1st Sam. 21:13). The ruse works and Achish has David ushered out (1st Sam. 21:14-15). David escapes back to Israel, where he will spend the next decade or more hiding in the Judean wilderness.

The Heart of David

All of his nights learning to sing to the hosts of heaven while watching the sheep will now be David's guide. Up to now, we have been largely guessing at David's thoughts and feelings. But starting from this point on, we have psalms that capture how David is thinking and feeling at each critical moment of his wilderness journey.

Psalm 56 captures the emotions of David's capture and release at Gath. According to the superscript above the psalm, David wrote this psalm just after the event:

> They stir up strife, they lurk; they watch my steps, as they have waited for my life. For their crime will they escape? In wrath cast down the peoples, O God! You have kept count of my tossings; put my tears in your bottle. Are they not in your book" (Ps. 56:6-8)?

Here it is easy to sense David's fear, how hunted he feels. You can also see his bitterness to those who have betrayed him. Oddly he never seems to direct bitterness against Saul. He shakes off all of his negative emotions to praise God and to tell God thank you for saving me. He doesn't for an instant imagine that his own cunning has saved his neck:

> In God, whose word I praise, in the LORD, whose word I praise, in God I trust; I shall not be afraid. What can man do to me? I must perform my vows to you, O God; I will render thank offerings to you. For you have delivered my soul from death, yes, my feet from falling, that I may walk before God in the light of life (Ps. 56:10-13).

Psalm 34 is also tagged as commemorating the same events. But in this psalm the fear and the anger have subsided. Instead, the psalm rings a jubilant tone from the start:

> I will bless the LORD at all times; his praise shall continually be in my mouth. My soul makes its boast in the LORD; let the humble hear and be glad. Oh, magnify

> the LORD with me, and let us exalt his name together! I sought the LORD, and he answered me and delivered me from all my fears (Ps. 34:1-4).

David escapes to the cave of Adullam. Here he hears the ugly news, which we read about in 1st Sam. ch. 22, Doeg the Edomite has informed Saul that David had received help from the priests of Nob. Saul calls the priests before him and confronts them. Of course, they have little to say since they didn't know that Saul was chasing David at the time. Never-the-less, Saul commands the guards to slay the priests, but the guards refuse (1st Sam. 22:17). Doeg then obliges Saul by killing 85 priests that day and he continued on to Nob where he killed men, women, children, even the livestock (1st Sam. 22:18-19), something he failed to do when confronting the Amalikites (1st Sam. 15:17-23). Abiathar, one of the sons of Ahimelech and a priest, has escaped to join David in the cave of Adullam. Crushed by the news, David mourns, "I knew on that day, when Doeg the Edomite was there, that he would surely tell Saul. I have occasioned the death of all the persons of your father's house. Stay with me; do not be afraid, for he who seeks my life seeks your life. With me you shall be in safekeeping" (1st Sam. 22:22-23). And so Abiathar becomes David's priest.

Psalm 52 shows the contempt that David has for Doeg and his actions. He contrasts Doeg's attitude with that of a godly man, and describes the results:

> Your tongue plots destruction, like a sharp razor, you worker of deceit. You love evil more than good, and lying more than speaking what is right (Ps. 52:2-3).

God will break you down forever (Ps. 52:5).

The righteous shall see and fear, and shall laugh at him, saying, "See the man who would not make God his refuge, but trusted in the abundance of his riches and sought refuge in his own destruction!" But I am like a green olive tree in the house of God. I trust in the steadfast love of God forever and ever (Ps. 52:6-8).

Discussion Points:

1. David prefers to think well of everyone. Why is he so angry with Doeg the Edomite, but not with Saul?

2. What is David's relationship with the men of God such as Samuel and the priests of Nob?

3. David is willing to speak out his emotions, good and bad. Why should his fear and anger be part of the Psalms?

4. Why does David feel so guilty in the death of the priests of Nob?

Application:

1. We see that David was highly incensed at the murder of the priests of Nob. He blamed Doeg the Edomite, who carried out the sentence when Saul's own guards would not. Still, David did not speak ill of Saul, even though it was Saul who ordered the murder of the priests. Are there people you are angry with? Why? Are there people you should be angry with, but are not? Why?

2. David was surrounded by many people who were not of the highest social standing. He didn't have a lot of choice in who came to follow him. Never-the-less, he did have his mighty men, and he had Abiathar, his priest. Who do you like to hang out with the most? Do they strengthen you or weaken you? When things get difficult, do you go to a different set of people?

3. David went to Nob never dreaming that his visit there would cause the death of all of the priests as well as their families. He feels guilty. Are there things in your life for which you feel guilty, though you had little control over the situation?

46. David in the Wilderness

CHAPTER 6: IN THE WILDERNESS

> And everyone who was in distress, and everyone who was in debt, and everyone who was bitter in soul, gathered to him. And he became commander over them. And there were with him about four hundred men (1st Sam. 22:2).

Keilah and the Philistines

Reading: 1st Samuel 23:1-14
Psalms 57, 63 & 142

Since hiding in Philistine territory proved nearly fatal, David returns to Israel. As we saw, he hides in "the cave of Adullam" (1 Samuel 22:1). There is considerable debate as to where this cave was, (the Hebrew could imply any stronghold). Some say near Bethlehem, as 2nd Sam. 23:13-17 relates the story of King David encamped at Adullam again. Three of his strong men break through Philistine lines to collect water from the well in Bethlehem. Most place location south of Jerusalem where there is a 'Tel (or hill) Adullam' overlooking the West Bank about fifteen miles south of Jerusalem.

Word got out that David was there, so many people gathered to him. Some were mighty warriors who had been serving under him, his family came, but also many who were angry or bitter, many who were fleeing debt burdens in a day when bankruptcy was not an option. His company swelled to four-hundred men, not including women and children. Before he would return from the wilderness, he would be leading six hundred men.

Despite questionable relationships within his natural family, David is careful to take care of his mother and father. He takes them to Mizpah and places them under the protection of the king of Moab (1st Sam. 22:3-4), we assume for a fee. When the prophet Gad comes to David and warns him to flee Adullam (1st Sam. 22:5), David packs up and begins his wilderness trials fleeing from one place to another, always trying to stay one step ahead of Saul. At the same time, David is attempting to protect many who are simply fleeing the fate of the priests of Nob. His force is not large enough to confront Saul's army, and David doesn't want to confront Saul, so he must run and hide. But with hundreds of mouths to feed, it is difficult for David to hide for long.

As if this is not enough, news comes to him: "the Philistines are fighting against Keilah and are plundering the threshing floors" (1st Sam. 23:1). He could have said, Saul is the king, he needs to take care of the issue; instead, he inquires of God, "Shall I go and attack these Philistines" (1st Sam. 23:2)? His men were already in fear of Saul, so to take their small force and intentionally attack a Philistine army seems foolish. They balk at the suggestion. David inquires again, and God says, "Arise, go down to Keilah, for I will give the Philistines into your hand." (1st Sam. 23:4).

There are several things that this passage makes clear. First is that David has a genuine concern for the people of Israel. His care for his people outweighs his concern for self-preservation. And, he immediately asks God for direction. When his men object, David asks God for confirmation. With that confirmation, he acts decisively. David and his small army route the Philistines and save Keilah (1st Sam. 23:5). Afterwards, David seeks God's council again and realizes that he must leave Keilah immediately.

The Negeb

David flees deeper into the Negeb, a barren land in the southern part of Israel. There are few trees here, and food and water are scarce. Moreover, raiding parties from neighboring tribes are frequent here. In the Negeb, David will begin to feel the full weight of his exile:

> Look to the right and see: there is none who takes notice of me; no refuge remains to me; no one cares for my soul. I cry to you, O LORD; I say, "You are my refuge, my portion in the land of the living." Attend to my cry, for I am brought very low! Deliver me from my persecutors, for they are too strong for me (Ps. 142:4-6)!

David's prayer rings out from "when he was in the cave" (Ps. 142:1).

David is not relying on any schemes he might concoct. He is declaring, "You [God] are my refuge" (Ps. 142:5). Psalm 63, written "when he was in the wilderness of Judah" (Ps. 63:1), clearly displays the longing of David's heart. It has become a favorite contemporary worship song. If we look at the circumstances in which David wrote this psalm, we will notice an intensity in it, that the lyric beauty of the psalm tends to mask:

> O God, you are my God; earnestly I seek you; my soul thirsts for you; my flesh faints for you, as in a dry and weary land where there is no water.
>
> So I have looked upon you in the sanctuary, beholding your power and glory.
>
> Because your steadfast love is better than life, my lips will praise you.
>
> So I will bless you as long as I live; in your name I will lift up my hands.
>
> My soul will be satisfied as with fat and rich food, and my mouth will praise you with joyful lips,
>
> when I remember you upon my bed, and meditate on you in the watches of the night
>
> for you have been my help, and in the shadow of your wings I will sing for joy.
>
> My soul clings to you; your right hand upholds me.
>
> But those who seek to destroy my life shall go down into the depths of the earth;
>
> they shall be given over to the power of the sword; they shall be a portion for jackals.
>
> But the king shall rejoice in God; all who swear by him shall exult, for the mouths of liars will be stopped (Ps. 63:1-11).

The first two verses voice an incredible longing for God's presence. This psalm matches Psalm 42 in many ways. That psalm starts with another memorable statement of longing: "As a deer pants for flowing streams, so pants my soul for you, O God. My soul thirsts for God, for the living God" (Ps. 42:1-2). Exiled to the Negeb, thirst seems to be an apt metaphor for his desperate situation. While most of us tend to ruminate Job-like for seeming ages, David follows the flow upward: "I have looked upon you," "beholding your power and glory," "my lips will praise you" (Ps. 63:2-3). And so, David launches into several verses of the most magnificent praise. In Psalm 42, the psalmist stops the flow to ask, "Why are you cast down, O my soul, and why are you in turmoil within me? Hope in God; for I shall again praise him, my salvation and my God. My soul is cast down within me; therefore I remember you from the land of Jordan and of Hermon, from Mount Mizar" (Ps. 42:5-6). Like Psalm 42, David moves effortlessly between laying his struggles before God and reaching upwards in praise. Psalm 63 sweeps us right along with him.

David continues to move higher in his devotions, he sees his own deliverance from woe: "My soul will be satisfied as with fat and rich food" (Ps. 63:5). This is no prosperity gospel, his vision is based on the firm foundation of his relationship with God, which is a tried and tested relationship. David is confident of God's help, because, as he states it, "you have been my help" (Ps. 63:7).

What we are seeing at work is David with a tried-and-true formula for overcoming the darkness from without that is attempting to work its way into his soul. I doubt he ever wrote this out as his five points to spiritual fitness. Rather this is a pattern that slipped under his skin on the many lonely nights when the cold and dark pressed about him, whispering rejection. He would pull out his harp and play a song for the LORD.

Psalm 57, also written “when he fled from Saul in the cave” (Ps. 57:1), exposes the warfare underneath. “Be merciful to me, O God, be merciful to me, for in you my soul takes refuge” (Ps. 57:1). He begins, “I cry out to God Most High, to God who fulfills his purpose for me” (Ps. 57:2). His gaze upwards allows him to shift into confident declaration: “He will send from heaven and save me” (Ps. 57:3). The psalm struggles back and forth: “My soul is in the midst of lions” (Ps. 57:4). “Be exalted, O God” (Psalm 57:5). “They set a net for my steps; my soul was bowed down. They dug a pit in my way, but they have fallen into it themselves” (Ps. 57:6). “My heart is steadfast, O God” (Psalm 57:7). And then we see him break through:

> Awake, my glory! Awake, O harp and lyre!
> I will awake the dawn!
>
> I will give thanks to you, O Lord, among the peoples; I will sing praises to you among the nations.
>
> For your steadfast love is great to the heavens, your faithfulness to the clouds.
>
> Be exalted, O God, above the heavens! Let your glory be over all the earth (Ps. 57:8-11)!

By this process of internal warfare, external praise, and remembering all the good that God has done for him so far, David is able to stir his soul so that he clearly sees his enemies defeated, as he sees God's care for him, “But the king shall rejoice in God; all who swear by him shall exult, for the mouths of liars will be stopped" (Ps. 63:11). At this point, I do not believe that David is affirming a creed or "standing on the word," He is declaring what his soul sees. This is all a part of his close relationship with God.

Discussion Points:

1. How is David's heart and/or anointing shown in his defense of Keilah?

2. Where does David go for advice?

3. When the men object out of fear, how does David deal with their fear?

4. Seeing Psalm 63 in the light of the circumstances he was under, how does that change your understanding of David and his psalm?

5. Who is David's closest friend in the wilderness?

Application:

1. Sometimes we feel prompted to do something, as David is prompted to defend Keila, but we don't necessarily know why. Perhaps, the urgency doesn't seem to come from us naturally. Is it possible that these are moments when the Holy Spirit is prompting you? Describe of a situation in your life that shows God's heart at work in and through you. These may be small acts or big ones.

2. In so many of the psalms, we see that David is afraid and oppressed. We see him reaching out to God for help, for direction, as well as for emotional support. Listening to the nightly news can stir up fear, if we don't have enough difficulty in our lives to stir fear up already. How do you deal with fear? When people around you are afraid, are you able to calm them?

3. We see that David overcomes his fears many times, by simply praising God. Even though his circumstances haven't changed, his mood had radically altered from one of anxiety to one of jubilance. Are you able to praise God in difficult circumstances?

56. David in the Wilderness

CHAPTER 7: SAUL'S LIFE

> And David said to Saul, "Why do you listen to the words of men who say, 'Behold, David seeks your harm?' Behold, this day your eyes have seen how the LORD gave you today into my hand in the cave. And some told me to kill you, but I spared you. I said, 'I will not put out my hand against my lord, for he is the LORD's anointed'" (1st Sam. 24:9-10).

Reading: 1st Samuel 24 & 26
Psalms 54 & 143

Potty Break

David spares Saul's life, not once, but twice. In chapter 24, Saul, who is pursuing David to kill him, enters a cave to relieve himself. He is alone and therefore quite vulnerable. Unaware that David and his men are hiding in this very cave (1st Sam. 24:3), Saul is an easy target. His men press David, apparently with his own words "Here is the day of which the LORD said to you, 'Behold, I will give your enemy into your hand, and you shall do to him as it shall seem good to you'" (1st Sam. 24:4).

A couple of things to remember here: God has never said He would give Saul into *David's* hand, and David has never asked for it. These men, moreover, are not the best of Israel's crop. Many of them have come to David out of desperation owing to financial or legal problems. They are tempted by a possible quick end to their problems. I sense that David is listening for God's voice. When he doesn't hear it, he is cautious.

David is in a dark and desperate place. He is not only being opposed, he is being hunted down, pursued with one purpose in mind: the death of David. Psalm 54, composed, according to the script at the top, when the Ziphites had informed Saul of David's location in the Negeb, concludes: "For he has delivered me from every trouble, and my eye has looked in triumph on my enemies" (Ps. 54:7). This could be what the men are referring to above. But, as mentioned, it does not give David permission to kill Saul. Of his adversaries, David says, "For strangers have risen against me; ruthless men seek my life; they do not set God before themselves" (Ps. 54:3).

In Psalm 143, a psalm of David, but not directly attached to a specific event, David says, "you will cut off my enemies" (Ps. 143:12), however, the NASB, states it more as a request, "in Your lovingkindness, cut off my enemies." This psalm does speak of sitting in darkness, which is the circumstance of the En Gedi cave where David is sitting in the above account. He adds, "the enemy has persecuted my soul" (Ps. 143:3, NASB). In his dire circumstances, David realizes that not only is his life in danger, but all of his thoughts and feelings are being pushed towards darkness.

Remember

The most remarkable aspect of David's personality is his ability to continually free his thoughts from the world in front of him and to look for God, both in past victories over tremendous difficulties, and in promises and prophecies. It is this aspect of David's personality that makes him a true leader loved by God. In the midst of very difficult circumstances, David is able see God's path ahead of him, and refuses to deviate from it, not even for a prophetic word repackaged to fit the needs of the moment.

> I remember the days of old; I meditate on all that you have done; I ponder the work of your hands (Ps. 143:5).

Although Psalm 143 doesn't specify which past events he is thinking about, David is telling God, in this psalm/prayer, 'I remember.' Is David remembering how the towering giant Goliath fell before him? One stone found its mark, while Goliath stood still mocking the boy. Or is David remembering how he eluded Saul's spear on more than one occasion? Why did King Achish let David go? How is it that in the moment that David was being pinned down in the wilderness of Ziph that Saul suddenly had to pull away to stop a Philistine attack? Search the word 'remember' in the Psalms, it is a theme which comes up again and again.

God's covenant is celebrated in what He has done. In this way, we can trust in our hope of what He will do. The future is informed by the past. We see this in the celebration of the first Passover celebration: "Then Moses said to the people, 'Remember this day in which you came out from Egypt, out of the house of slavery, for by a strong hand the LORD brought you out from this place'" (Exo. 13:3). When Jesus was about to face capture and a torturous death, he sits down to eat: "And he took bread, and when he had given thanks, he broke it and gave it to them, saying, 'This is my body, which is given for you. Do this in remembrance of me'" (Luke 22:19). The promises are made concrete not by our imagination, but by remembering what has already been done for us.

The Passover and the Eucharist bread and wine are large scale covenant celebrations. Within these larger covenants are our individual relationships with God. Every Jew and every Christian has the ability to draw near to God. How? Calling on God in prayer and fasting. Finding God's heart in the Bible and in putting into practice the actions which win God's heart: mercy, kindness, justice and so on; resisting the voices, loud and many, to compromise, try a little perversion, a little rebellion, do your own thing. In this way, small miracles begin to pile up. Someone is strengthened who had no hope. A life is changed. A catastrophe is averted. Peace comes in a fearful situation. Whatever happens, notice when God shows up, and *remember*. Remember that God hears you, and God responds. God has a relationship with the body of Christ, with godly nations, but God also has a relationship with every living soul that has breath, and that means you. Covet that relationship and deepen it, by personal interaction and by remembrance. This is what we see David doing time and time again.

> Let me hear in the morning of your steadfast love, for in you I trust. Make me know the way I should go, for to you I lift up my soul (Ps. 143:8).

David is not remembering the bad times or the things that have been said or done against him. These do not lift him up and encourage him. He is not remembering the adversary's hand; he is remembering God's hand in his life.

The second encouragement that David has is that several prophecies have been spoken over him. First, he was anointed by Samuel (1st Sam. 16:12-13). The meaning was clear. When God tells him to go, Samuel protests, "If Saul hears it, he will kill me" (1st Sam. 16:2). So, he travels under pretenses, anoints David in front of his family alone, and quickly leaves (1st Sam. 16:13). The need for secrecy and the fear surrounding Samuel's visit shows that this was not a simple 'impartation.' Scripture says that "the Spirit of the LORD rushed upon David from that day forward" (1st Sam. 16:13). David's awareness of God, and of his own destiny in God were magnified from that day on.

Most remarkable is that Jonathan, the son of King Saul and the heir apparent, knows that God is with David. He has already made a covenant with David because of it: "do not cut off your steadfast love from my house forever, when the LORD cuts off every one of the enemies of David from the face of the earth" (1st Sam. 20:15). Jonathan comes to David in the wilderness to "strengthened his hand in God" (1st Sam. 23:16). How? Jonathan prophesies over David, "Do not fear, for the hand of Saul my father shall not find you. You shall be king over Israel, and I shall be next to you. Saul my father also knows this" (1st Sam. 23:17). Jonathan, as heir apparent, would not be disposed to believing that David would be the next king, but he does, and he comes to David to pledge his support.

So here is David: he is running and hiding in a barren and inhospitable land with little food or water. He has a band of six-hundred misfits and social rejects. Pursuing him is a well-trained, well-armed, and a well-supplied army of three thousand chosen men who have lookouts everywhere. His situation looks hopeless. On the other hand, he knows that God has been protecting him, and further, he has every reason to believe that God wants to make him king over Israel. In this dilemma, suddenly David finds Saul right in front of him, inches from the tip of his blade, caught literally with his pants down (1st Sam. 24:3).

Does he put an end to Saul right now? Jonathan, Saul's son, has said the "the LORD cuts off every one of the enemies of David," and all his men know that God's word to David is, "Behold, I will give your enemy into your hand, and you shall do to him as it shall seem good to you" (1st Sam. 24:4). Saul is definitely an enemy to David. Why should David hesitate?

There is only one explanation, it doesn't feel right. In the midst of this highly charged moment, David pauses and breathes, "Answer me quickly, O LORD! My spirit fails" (Ps. 143:7)! He rises and quietly cuts off the edge of Saul's robe (1st Sam. 24:4). He has promised himself to Saul, and even now refuses to betray that trust.

This event runs parallel to Samuel's prophecy over Saul. Because of Saul's disobedience to the word of the LORD, Samuel prophecies that Saul has been rejected by God. When Samuel turns to leave, Saul grabs Samuel's robe and it tears. Samuel prophecies, "The LORD has torn the kingdom of Israel from you this day and has given it to a neighbor of yours, who is better than you" (1st Sam. 15:28).

When Saul and his army have moved away some distance, David calls out, while holding the edge of Saul's robe to display his lack of ill-will towards Saul (1st Sam. 24:8). "Is this your voice, my son David" (1st Sam. 24:16)? Saul, it says, lifted up his voice and wept. He calls to David,

> "You are more righteous than I, for you have repaid me good, whereas I have repaid you evil. And you have declared this day how you have dealt well with me, in that you did not kill me when the LORD put me into your hands. For if a man finds his enemy, will he let him go away safe? So may the LORD reward you with good for what you have done to me this day. And now, behold, I know that you shall surely be king, and that the kingdom of Israel shall be established in your hand. Swear to me therefore by the LORD that you will not cut off my offspring after me, and that you will not destroy my name out of my father's house" (1st Sam. 24:17-21).

A Deep Sleep

Saul does not keep his word. He is soon back pursuing David. In an even more remarkable way, the scene from En Gedi repeats itself. David and one of his mighty men approach Saul's army at night. All three thousand soldiers are in a deep sleep, which allows David to walk into the camp and right up to where Saul lies sleeping. His friend Abishai tells David, "God has given your enemy into your hand this day. Now please let me pin him to the earth with one stroke of the spear, and I will not strike him twice" (1st Sam. 26:8). David is immediate in his reply, "Do not destroy him, for who can put out his hand against the LORD's anointed and be guiltless" (1st Sam. 26:9)?

David continues, "As the LORD lives, the LORD will strike him, or his day will come to die, or he will go down into battle and perish. The LORD forbid that I should put out my hand against the LORD's anointed. But take now the spear that is at his head and the jar of water, and let us go" (1st Sam. 26:10-11). Since his last encounter, David has had time to mull over his response and is now quick and decisive. He knows his answer ahead of time. Abishai seems to be aware of David's response and offers to dispatch Saul himself.

Discussion Points:

1. How does David show his value for God's anointing?

2. Why does David refuse to take things in his own hands?

3. How do we see David rely on the LORD?

4. What memories of God's help for him personally can David call upon?

5. What are the promises of God that David can rely upon?

Application:

1. We see that David had the temptation to take things into his own hands and kill Saul. He has the foresight to resist the temptation. Are you tempted to take things into your own hands at times? Think of a specific incidence. How did you react? How do you think you can you rely on the LORD more?

2. When you look back over your life, are there times that you can see God was at work on your behalf? Are there moments that you can remember of a special closeness with God? Do you think to recall those memories in times of difficult circumstances?

3. David had many times when those around him have affirmed his destiny. Are there trusted people in your life who have spoken words over you that you can use to remember and encourage yourself in difficult times? Are there specific promises of God for you, that you can rely upon?

CHAPTER 8: WISE COUNSEL

> And when the LORD has done to my lord according to all the good that he has spoken concerning you and has appointed you prince over Israel, my lord shall have no cause of grief or pangs of conscience for having shed blood without cause or for my lord working salvation himself. And when the LORD has dealt well with my lord, then remember your servant (1st Sam. 25:30-31).

Reading: 1st Samuel 25
Psalm 51

A Wise Woman

We have already seen that David was surrounded by social rejects, misfits, criminals and debtors. Their counsel was not trustworthy. David relied on his prayers to God, as well as inquiries to the ephod that Ahimelech had brought when he fled Saul (1st Sam. 23:6-12). But David was a man of action. He occasionally went into action before he had stopped to think through the results or to inquire of the LORD. This is abundantly clear in the incident in the wilderness with Nabal and Abigail.

As the story unfolds, David, besides running from Saul, has also been protecting the settlements in the wilderness of Judah, the Negeb. It was the time of sheep shearing and David heard that a wealthy man by the name of Nabal was shearing sheep with his men. David sent some of his young men to ask for food from Nabal (1st Sam. 25:5-9). "And Nabal answered David's servants, 'Who is David? Who is the son of Jesse? There are many servants these days who are breaking away from their masters. Shall I take my bread and my water and my meat that I have killed for my shearers and give it to men who come from I do not know where'" (1st Sam. 25:10-11)? Nabal has just accused David of rebellion, which is untrue, and unwisely insulted a man with an army of 600 men. Even if David's men are largely misfits, they are now a seasoned fighting force. Moreover, there are several exceptional warriors with him, David's mighty men (1st Chron. 11:10-47).

When Nabal's reply is relayed to David, his answer is quick: "Every man strap on his sword" (1st Sam. 25:13)! David and 400 of his men march towards Nabal's encampment, whose servants know that this will not end well for them, and so they tell the situation to Abigail, Nabal's wife:

> "Behold, David sent messengers out of the wilderness to greet our master, and he railed at them. Yet the men were very good to us, and we suffered no harm, and we did not miss anything when we were in the fields, as long as we went with them. They were a wall to us both by night and by day, all the while we were with them keeping

> the sheep. Now therefore know this and consider what you should do, for harm is determined against our master and against all his house, and he is such a worthless man that one cannot speak to him" (1st Sam. 25:14-17).

Abigail immediately loads a large store of provisions on donkeys and sends servants ahead to announce her coming. She, herself, comes with the gift. David is steamed to say the least: "Surely in vain have I guarded all that this fellow has in the wilderness, so that nothing was missed of all that belonged to him, and he has returned me evil for good. God do so to the enemies of David and more also, if by morning I leave so much as one male of all who belong to him" (1st Sam. 25:21-22).

Abigail arrives and gets down from her donkey, she bows low before David, she begins to apologize and to reason with David:

> "On me alone, my lord, be the guilt. Please let your servant speak in your ears, and hear the words of your servant. Let not my lord regard this worthless fellow, Nabal, for as his name is, so is he. Nabal is his name, and folly is with him. But I your servant did not see the young men of my lord, whom you sent. Now then, my lord, as the LORD lives, and as your soul lives, because the LORD has restrained you from bloodguilt and from saving with your own hand, now then let your enemies and those who seek to do evil to my lord be as Nabal. And now let this present that your servant has brought

> to my lord be given to the young men who follow my lord. Please forgive the trespass of your servant.
>
> For the LORD will certainly make my lord a sure house, because my lord is fighting the battles of the LORD, and evil shall not be found in you so long as you live. If men rise up to pursue you and to seek your life, the life of my lord shall be bound in the bundle of the living in the care of the LORD your God. And the lives of your enemies he shall sling out as from the hollow of a sling.
>
> And when the LORD has done to my lord according to all the good that he has spoken concerning you and has appointed you prince over Israel, my lord shall have no cause of grief or pangs of conscience for having shed blood without cause or for my lord working salvation himself. And when the LORD has dealt well with my lord, then remember your servant (1st Sam. 25:24-31).

David hears Abigail's plea. He immediately recognizes that she speaks with great wisdom. It's as if the recently departed prophet Samuel had come back to life to give him counsel. "Blessed be the LORD, the God of Israel, who sent you this day to meet me! Blessed be your discretion, and blessed be you, who have kept me this day from bloodguilt and from working salvation with my own hand! For as surely as the LORD, the God of Israel, lives, who has restrained me from hurting you, unless you had hurried and come to meet me, truly by morning there had not been left to Nabal so much as one male" (1st Sam. 25:32-34). He receives Abigail's gift and turns his troop around.

It does not end well for Nabal. When Abigail returns to tell him what has transpired, Nabal is inebriated so she waits. When the sun rises on her hungover husband, she tells him what has transpired. Nabal is in shock, literally. "In the morning, when the wine had gone out of Nabal, his wife told him these things, and his heart died within him, and he became as a stone" (1st Sam. 25:37). Ten days later, he dies. "When David heard that Nabal was dead, he said, 'Blessed be the LORD who has avenged the insult I received at the hand of Nabal, and has kept back his servant from wrongdoing. The LORD has returned the evil of Nabal on his own head.' Then David sent and spoke to Abigail, to take her as his wife" (1st Sam. 25:39).

So, Abigail becomes David's wife. Now stop and think about this situation. David is worked up emotionally, and with hundreds of men in his company he sets out to remove his reproach. But he is met by a woman who convinces him that he is on the wrong track. He changes his mind and withdraws. David is living in a patriarchal society. He, the leader, has been stopped in his tracks by a woman. He recognizes the wisdom in Abigail's argument, and humbles himself to it. With 400 pairs of eyes on him, David says thank you for stopping me. The men could let that pass, since they did get a large peace offering. Myself, when confronted, I think I would have difficulty humbling myself if there was only one witness. David goes beyond that; he takes this woman as his wife. How do his men reconcile this in their minds? Has she beguiled him?

A Love of Wisdom

Looking over the life of David, we notice several things which are at work here. One is that David is not particularly concerned with his image. He seems to be unaware of just how highly those around him think of him. What is important is his relationship with God. And he knows that his worship will bring respect from God's people. Notice his answer to Michal, Saul's daughter who sneers at his "shamelessly" dancing before the LORD: "It was before the LORD, who chose me above your father and above all his house, to appoint me as prince over Israel, the people of the LORD—and I will celebrate before the LORD. I will make myself yet more contemptible than this, and I will be abased in your eyes. But by the female servants of whom you have spoken, by them I shall be held in honor" (2nd Sam. 6:21-22).

Secondly, David respects wise counsel and keeps wise advisors around him. When David flees from the rebellion of his own son Absalom, it is told to him that a particular counselor Ahithophel has gone over to the rebellion. David prays, "O LORD, please turn the counsel of Ahithophel into foolishness" (2nd Sam. 15:31). Cleverly, David sends his loyal friend and counselor, Hushai the Archite to subvert the counsel of Ahithophel (2nd Sam. 15:34). Oddly, this rebellion was facilitated when David listened to the counsel of a "wise woman of Tekoa", who is put to the task by Joab, (the top commander who defects to Absolom), resulting in Absalom's restoration to royal privilege (2nd Sam. 14:1-21). Hindsight being 20-20, the counsel seems to have been unwise. The important point is that David keeps wise and godly men and women around him intentionally.

And finally, David's respect for truth before God causes him to humble himself before Nathan the prophet when he is confronted over his sin regarding Bathsheba. When Samuel had a word of rebuke for Saul, he had to leave Saul's presence for fear (1st Sam. 15:35). When God tells Samuel to go and anoint David, Samuel protests, "How can I go? If Saul hears it, he will kill me" (1st Sam. 16:2). It was dangerous to rebuke Saul.

David, on the other hand, welcomed Godly counsel whether it was to his liking or not. Nathan had ready access to David. In the 12th chapter of 2nd Samuel, Nathan appears with a stinging rebuke from the LORD complete with the pronouncement of God's curses (vs.1-12). David doesn't miss a beat, "I have sinned against the LORD" (2nd Sam. 12:13). "Create in me a clean heart, O God, and renew a right spirit within me" (Ps. 51:10). According to the superscription above verse 1, this psalm is, "A Psalm of David, when Nathan the prophet went to him, after he had gone in to Bathsheba." The psalm flows with contrition: "Behold, I was brought forth in iniquity, and in sin did my mother conceive me" (Ps. 51:5). David understands, "Behold, you delight in truth in the inward being, and you teach me wisdom in the secret heart" (Ps. 51:6). He has violated the truth set in his inward being and moved against the wisdom set in his heart. David has no quarrel with Nathan, his quarrel is with God, for which he can only ask for mercy. David sees the truth and honors it.

Discussion Points:

1. How difficult was it for David to humble himself to Abigail in front of men?

2. Why did David put such a high priority on having wise councilors around him?

3. How did David remain teachable?

4. David's reaction to strong rebuke is radically different than that of Saul. Why do you suppose that is?

Application:

1. We see David in a situation where Nabal has made him murderously angry. Abigail speaks wisdom to David, calming him and causing him to humble himself and change course. Think of a time when it was difficult for you to humble yourself? How well did you do?

2. David immediately recognized that Abigail was a wise councilor. When Nabal dies suddenly, David takes her as his wife. Later, when David is king, he especially values the council of specific men. Do you have wise councilors in your life?

3. We see that David is able to be taught by the wife of the man he is on his way to murder. We also see that Nathan and others are able to speak to him and he listens, even when the message is a bitter. How teachable are you? What attitudes can you cultivate to help you to become more teachable?

CHAPTER 9: THE DARKEST HOUR

> Answer me quickly, O LORD! My spirit fails! Hide not your face from me, lest I be like those who go down to the pit. Let me hear in the morning of your steadfast love, for in you I trust. Make me know the way I should go, for to you I lift up my soul (Ps. 143:7-8).

Reading: 1st Samuel chapters 27, 29 & 30:1-20

Psalm 143

They Want to Stone Me

The darkest hour is just before dawn. This old phrase is the perfect description of David's wilderness troubles. David has been in the wilderness running from Saul for more than a decade and there seems to be no let up. He decides, "Now I shall perish one day by the hand of Saul. There is nothing better for me than that I should escape to the land of the Philistines. Then Saul will despair of seeking me any longer within the borders of Israel, and I shall escape out of his hand" (1st Sam. 27:1). Things are pretty hopeless when the safest place to be is under the protection of Achish, king of Gath, from whom he had fled ten years earlier. But there goes David with his band of men. Achish grants him the town of Ziklag to dwell in (1st Sam. 27:6).

To make his presence palatable to the Philistine king, David convinces him that he is raiding Israelite villages, when in fact he is raiding anything but Israelite villages (1st Sam. 27:8-12). This becomes a problem. When the Philistines decide to make war on Israel (1st Sam. 28:1), David must agree to go up to battle alongside Achish, against Israel.

As the Philistine troops pass in review before the Philistine commanders, there is David with his 600 men. The commanders were angry with Achish and insisted that David and his men be sent back to Ziklag (1st Sam. 29:3-7). The Philistines have not forgotten the refrain, “Saul has struck down his thousands, and David his ten thousands” (1st Sam. 29:5). This, they know, refers to Philistine dead. In case David was not feeling insecure enough, now his presence with the Philistines is exposed, his welcome is likely to be withdrawn.

But wait, it gets even worse. “Now when David and his men came to Ziklag on the third day, the Amalekites had made a raid against the Negeb and against Ziklag. They had overcome Ziklag and burned it with fire and taken captive the women and all who were in it, both small and great. They killed no one, but carried them off and went their way” (1st Sam. 30:1-2). David's story is starting to look like Job's.

David's misery is compounded when the blame isn't focused on the Amalekites, but on him: “And David was greatly distressed, for the people spoke of stoning him, because all the people were bitter in soul, each for his sons and daughters” (1st Sam. 30:6). This is the place for all those cute aphorisms: ‘down to zero’, ‘lower than snail slime’, and so on. Sayings such as these are meant to blunt the sting, but imagine the turmoil in his heart. I've been in this sort of turmoil. It's impossible to sleep. In my case, I just crouched in the corner all night long. 'Slough of despond' doesn't begin to capture the despair. But…

David Strengthens Himself

"But David strengthened himself in the LORD his God" (1st Sam. 30:6). With this short phrase, David rises above his dire circumstance. His relationship with God is so close, that in the midst of earthly desolation, he never feels alone. He has somewhere to go and receive strength and refreshing. The only insight we can get as to what this strengthening might have looked like is from the psalms of David. In this case, we do not have a specific psalm to reference. We have seen him strengthen himself previously as in Psalm 63. In this instance, Psalm 143 appears to be an excellent model for what this strengthening might have looked like:

> Hear my prayer, O LORD; give ear to my pleas for mercy! In your faithfulness answer me, in your righteousness
>
> Enter not into judgment with your servant, for no one living is righteous before you
>
> For the enemy has pursued my soul; he has crushed my life to the ground; he has made me sit in darkness like those long dead.
>
> Therefore my spirit faints within me; my heart within me is appalled.

> I remember the days of old; I meditate on all that you have done; I ponder the work of your hands.
>
> I stretch out my hands to you; my soul thirsts for you like a parched land. *Selah.*
>
> Answer me quickly, O LORD! My spirit fails! Hide not your face from me, lest I be like those who go down to the pit.
>
> Let me hear in the morning of your steadfast love, for in you I trust. Make me know the way I should go, for to you I lift up my soul.
>
> Deliver me from my enemies, O LORD! I have fled to you for refuge.
>
> Teach me to do your will, for you are my God! Let your good Spirit lead me on level ground!
>
> For your name's sake, O LORD, preserve my life! In your righteousness bring my soul out of trouble!
>
> And in your steadfast love you will cut off my enemies, and you will destroy all the adversaries of my soul, for I am your servant (Ps. 143:1-12).

This psalm seems to move through three separate phases. The first four verses state the issues troubling David. There is no whining or going into endless detail, he simply states the general problem. Secondly, starting with, "I remember the days of old," David brings to remembrance the goodness of God for him during difficult times. There is a pause (*Selah*). And only then does David petition God for strength, for help from on high, and for wisdom and direction.

This last section, isn't just a petition, but it seems to move from despondence to confidence as it progresses. Having laid a foundation of placing the problem before God, and lifting up a praise to God for all the help He has provided in the past, David begins to pray with gathering energy.

We know, however this strengthening may have looked, it had the right effect. Immediately David is able to snap into action:

> And David said to Abiathar the priest, the son of Ahimelech, "Bring me the ephod." So Abiathar brought the ephod to David. And David inquired of the LORD, "Shall I pursue after this band? Shall I overtake them?" He answered him, "Pursue, for you shall surely overtake and shall surely rescue" (1st Sam. 30:7-8).

Clear thinking and confidence change the desperate atmosphere instantly. Talk of stoning David is shelved. David and all 600 men set out to pursue the Amalekites. They overtake the raiders and decimate them. Every captive is recovered. All of their stolen goods are recovered as well as the plunder from numerous other raids (1st Sam. 30:9-20).

Discussion Points:

1. How difficult must it have been for David to keep from becoming depressed and defeated?

2. What do you think it looked like when David strengthens himself in God?

3. Can you imagine David sitting before the Lord, feeling the full weight of his circumstances, to pray Psalm 143?

4. How did David change the atmosphere around him, when the men still wanted to stone him?

Application:

1. When David seems to have hit rock bottom, he strengthens himself in the Lord. Have you ever felt depressed and defeated? How did you get out of that feeling? Do you know how to strengthen yourself in God? What does that look like for you?

2. The circumstances in which David goes to strengthen himself in the Lord couldn't have been worse. But, after David has his talk with God, he consults Abiathar and gets definite direction from on high. The men immediately fall in behind David. Have you been in places or situations where the atmosphere seemed toxic? Was there anything you could do to change the atmosphere? Did the atmosphere change?

3. Looking at Psalm 143, which is clearly a prayer, how do your prayers begin? Are things you wish to change?

84. David in the Wilderness

CHAPTER 10: DEFEAT AND VICTORY

He sent from on high, he took me; he drew me out of many waters. He rescued me from my strong enemy and from those who hated me, for they were too mighty for me. They confronted me in the day of my calamity, but the LORD was my support. He brought me out into a broad place; he rescued me, because he delighted in me (Ps. 18:16-19).

My Misery is Gone

Reading: 1st Samuel 30:20-31
2nd Samuel 1 & 2:1-11

In victory, David does not exalt. One third of the men had been too exhausted to continue on to the final battle. Remember that many of those who follow David are societies least desirable, "wicked and worthless fellows." These men suggest to David, "Because they did not go with us, we will not give them any of the spoil that we have recovered, except that each man may lead away his wife and children, and depart" (1st Sam. 30:22). David is firm: "You shall not do so, my brothers, with what the LORD has given us. He has preserved us and given into our hand the band that came against us. Who would listen to you in this matter? For as his share is who goes down into the battle, so shall his share be who stays by the baggage. They shall share alike" (1st Sam. 30:23-24).

David is also generous beyond his little band of men. When he returns to Ziklag, he immediately sends a part of the spoil to the elders of Judah, as well as to all of those towns and cities where he had the occasion to find himself in his times of trouble (1st Sam. 30:26-31).

The Song of the Bow

Saul and Jonathan are not so fortunate. The battle with the Philistines goes badly. Saul, Jonathan, and two other sons of Saul, are overtaken and killed. On the one hand, this is good news for David. His troubles are over and he is now able to return to Israel. But David seems to ignore that completely. This is bad news for Israel who has been defeated at the hand of the Philistines. Saul and David's good friend Jonathan are dead, and the Philistine's exalt over their victory. In this account, the Amalekite who brought the news to David claims to have killed Saul at his own request (2nd Sam. 1:2-13). David is indignant, "How is it you were not afraid to put out your hand to destroy the LORD's anointed" (2nd Sam. 1:14)? David orders him to be killed immediately (2nd Sam. 1:15).

And so, David regrets the fall of Saul and Jonathan as the fall of great warriors fallen in battle. "The Song of the Bow" is David's lament for Saul and Jonathan, which he commanded to be taught to all of Judah:

> Your glory, O Israel, is slain on your high places! How the mighty have fallen!

Tell it not in Gath, publish it not in the streets of Ashkelon, lest the daughters of the Philistines rejoice, lest the daughters of the uncircumcised exult.

You mountains of Gilboa, let there be no dew or rain upon you, nor fields of offerings! For there the shield of the mighty was defiled, the shield of Saul, not anointed with oil.

From the blood of the slain, from the fat of the mighty, the bow of Jonathan turned not back, and the sword of Saul returned not empty.

Saul and Jonathan, beloved and lovely! In life and in death they were not divided; they were swifter than eagles; they were stronger than lions.

You daughters of Israel, weep over Saul, who clothed you luxuriously in scarlet, who put ornaments of gold on your apparel.

How the mighty have fallen in the midst of the battle! Jonathan lies slain on your high places.

I am distressed for you, my brother Jonathan; very pleasant have you been to me; your love to me was extraordinary, surpassing the love of women.

How the mighty have fallen, and the weapons of war perished (2nd Sam. 1:19-27)!

David and Jonathan had a special relationship. They had become close like brothers. The years of Saul's anger does not seem to have fractured that bond.

But Saul's relation to David is complex, to say the least. In some ways, he was like a surrogate father to David. But then, he becomes a murderous foe, devoting a huge number of resources, and years of effort, in an attempt to track down and kill David. Despite this, as we discussed in previous chapters, David never considers Saul to be his enemy.

There is another factor here. David has a special reverence for the Lord's anointing. We see this when he orders the Amalekite slain (2nd Sam. 1:14-15). We know that he has the Lord's anointing on himself, and it is particularly active in his life. So, a part of David's reverence may be a recognition of God's Hand in selecting and appointing Saul. Even though the anointing seems to have departed from Saul a long time ago, David retains his respect for Saul's anointing to the very end.

Discussion Points:

1. After so many years of deprivation, David insists on generosity with their good fortune. How is it that he can part with the sudden wealth?

2. David does not exalt over Saul's death, but rather pays him a great deal of respect. Why do you think he is so gracious to the man who tried to kill him?

3. Why does David write a special psalm for Saul and Jonathan, and why does he require it to be taught to all the people of Judah (2nd Sam. 1:18)?

4. Even though the Lord took the anointing off of Saul (1st Sam. 16:14), David still respects the anointing that had been on Saul. Why?

Application:

1. David has a rag to riches moment almost overnight. He is able to transition from being the hunted rebel, to being the king. Have you ever had difficult times, followed by easy times? If so, how did it affect your behavior?

2. David remains respectful to his former adversary. In fact, he goes to great lengths to honor the memory of Saul. When you have a great breakthrough or win a great honor, how do you act? How do you treat former adversaries who have been defeated? Does something specific come to mind?

3. David has a great deal of respect for the Lord's anointing, even for those who have fallen from grace. Think of those in ministry who have fallen from grace, how do you think of them? Are you able to honor them for the good they did?

CHAPTER 11: THE FACE OF GOD

> After this David inquired of the LORD, "Shall I go up into any of the cities of Judah?" And the LORD said to him, "Go up." David said, "To which shall I go up?" And he said, "To Hebron." So David went up there, and his two wives also, Ahinoam of Jezreel and Abigail the widow of Nabal of Carmel. And David brought up his men who were with him, everyone with his household, and they lived in the towns of Hebron. And the men of Judah came, and there they anointed David king over the house of Judah (2nd Sam. 2:1-4).

The King of Judah

Reading: 2nd Samuel 1:19-27 & 2:1-7
Psalm 18

It would be good to review and re-examine some of the things which make David the obvious candidate as replacement for Saul. While Saul had spent a great deal of time hunting down his greatest general in order to kill him, David was continually hunting down the raiding parties which plagued Judah.

While Saul levied taxes and conscripted young men to harass him, David was quick to share the spoil taken from large raiding parties. David was a continual blessing to Judah even in the midst of his trials. David was a mighty warrior, with a reputation greater than that of Saul. It didn't hurt that David was of the tribe of Judah, whereas Saul was a Benjamite.

It seemed obvious to many people that David was destined to be the king. We hear that from Abigail (1st Sam. 25:30). But more importantly, Jonathan, the heir apparent, encourages David and prophecies that David will be king (1st Sam. 23:17). We assume that Samuel's anointing of David was never public knowledge, but Samuel's public rebuke of Saul was well known: "The LORD has torn the kingdom of Israel from you this day and has given it to a neighbor of yours, who is better than you. And also the Glory of Israel will not lie or have regret, for he is not a man, that he should have regret" (1st Sam. 15:28-29). Even the Philistines call David the "king of the land" (1st Sam. 21:11).

But this is all the view from the world's vantage point. Politics was running in David's favor. Heaven's view favors David as well, but for very different reasons. God has anointed David through Samuel as we know. Saul used his position as king to his own advantage, and never cultivated the anointing. In contrast, David has stepped into his anointing even though he is not yet king. As Abigail states it: "For the LORD will certainly make my lord a sure house, because my lord is fighting the battles of the LORD, and evil shall not be found in you so long as you live" (1st Sam. 25:28).

We saw that already in the confrontation with Goliath, David's perspective of the situation was very different from any one else around him. He saw the battle as the Lord's battle and the people of Israel as the Lord's people. A threat against Israel was a challenge to God directly. David's personal concerns became small in light of national concerns and especially God's concern. We see this also when the Philistines are attacking Keilah, David's heart is immediately to go and to rescue this town. He inquires of the LORD and determines to go despite the fears and objections of his men (1st Sam. 23:1-5).

David, the giant slayer, inspired great warriors. His patriotic and Godly vision gave purpose to the battle. 1st Chron. 11:10-12:40 lists the warriors who surrounded David in the wilderness and helped to establish him when he became king. It should be obvious that many of these men would never have become great without the inspiration of David leading them. The list starts with Jashobeam who killed three hundred men in a single battle. Abishai did the same (1st Chron. 11:20). Benaiah killed a giant (1st Chron. 11:23). As David's kingdom is established his warriors will kill several more giants. There is nothing like a giant slayer to inspire giant slayers.

David listened to advice and kept the best advisors around him, but when the advice he got didn't seem right, or the issue was too important to decide lightly, he always sought the Chief Advisor. Time and time again we see David calling for the Ephod or getting apart to 'refresh himself in the LORD.' He knew that some things only God could answer. David trusted that he would get the right answer if he sought God's will. Even in the matter of whether or not to leave the territory of the Philistine's and to return to Judah after the death of Saul, David asked God, "Shall I go up into any of the cities of Judah," and if so, "To which shall I go up" (2nd Sam. 2:1)? Given the circumstances, would we have even thought to ask?

Live Well in the Wilderness

David's attitude, his anointing, his willingness to listen to advise, even harsh advice, and David's quickness to inquire into God's advice all stem from one thing: David's relationship with God. This is seen in the psalms, many of which we have seen were written in David's dark days in the wilderness. In complaint, in fear, in anger and upset, David always stayed close to God. He always believed that God was his friend.

From the beginning of David's trial in the wilderness we see his heart displayed in the Psalms. David flees unprepared and without clear plans. His first stop, as we saw, was a visit to the priests of Nob who helped him on his way. Unfortunately, Doeg the Edomite sees David there and runs to tell Saul who kills all but one of the priests. In Psalm 52, David has harsh words for Doeg actions, but finishes the psalm by refocusing on his relationship with God: "But I am like a green olive tree in the house of God. I trust in the steadfast love of God forever and ever. I will thank you forever, because you have done it. I will wait for your name, for it is good, in the presence of the godly" (Ps. 52:8-9).

Soon, David finds himself in trouble in Gath where the Philistines have recognized him. He manages to escape, but his problems haven't gone away. He admits to feeling watched and hunted (Ps. 56:1-2, 5-6) and to fear (Ps. 56:3). I can almost see him in prayer, behind a bush, rocking and praying in the peculiar way Jews do:

> In God, whose word I praise, in the LORD, whose word I praise, in God I trust; I shall not be afraid. What can man do to me? I must perform my vows to you, O God; I

> will render thank offerings to you. For you have delivered my soul from death, yes, my feet from falling, that I may walk before God in the light of life (Ps. 56:10-13).

The notes proceeding the psalms tell us that both Psalm 56 as with Psalm 34 were written in response to David's brush with death in Gath. Psalm 56 has the urgency of someone whose heart is still beating fast. Psalm 34 reads like he has had time to calm down and reflect. In it, David soars lyric in his celebration of what God has done. There are great lines that have leant themselves to song: "Oh, taste and see that the LORD is good" (Ps. 34:8), and "Those who look to him are radiant, and their faces shall never be ashamed" (Ps. 34:5). In other words, the more David thinks about it, the happier he gets, until he just has to sing. David has not suddenly wandered onto easy street. He is simply seeing that God is there with him, protecting him.

His trials in the wilderness will continue for another 12 or 13 years. During this time, he writes several more psalms some of which are notated as having been written during this period. Psalm 54 is short thank you for rescue: "I will give thanks to Your name, O LORD, for it is good" (Ps. 54:6). Psalm 57 shows how he is making spiritual warfare: "My heart is steadfast, O God, my heart is steadfast! I will sing and make melody! Awake, my glory! Awake, O harp and lyre! I will awake the dawn! I will give thanks to you, O Lord, among the peoples; I will sing praises to you among the nations" (Ps. 57:7-9). And what can be said about Psalm 63. Three thousand years later, it makes a great worship song: "O God, you are my God; earnestly I seek you; my soul thirsts for you; my flesh faints for you, as in a dry and weary land where there is no water" (Ps. 63:1). And finally, Psalm 142 is a woeful prayer at a particularly difficult time: "Attend to my cry, for I am brought very low" (Psalm 142:6)! Dozens more of the psalms of David read as if they were also written during his time in the wilderness, or on remembering those times.

Remembering

There are two psalms of special interest at the moment when David's time of trial in the wilderness has ended. One the Song of the Bow, which David instructed be taught to all of Judah (2nd Sam. 1:18), and Psalm 18, a psalm written after Saul has died and David returns to Israel.

Let's look at Psalm 18 first. It has none of the wild and honest emotionalism of the psalms written in the wilderness. It could well have been written as an inaugural statement upon taking the throne of Judah: "You delivered me from strife with the people; you made me the head of the nations; people whom I had not known served me" (Ps. 18:43); and "Great salvation he brings to his king, and shows steadfast love to his anointed, to David and his offspring forever" (Ps. 18:50). The poetry is grand: "The LORD is my rock and my fortress and my deliverer, my God, my rock, in whom I take refuge, my shield, and the horn of my salvation, my stronghold" (Ps. 18:2). "Then the earth reeled and rocked; the foundations also of the mountains trembled and quaked, because he was angry" (Ps. 18:7). "For by you I can run against a troop, and by my God I can leap over a wall" (Ps. 18:29). "He made my feet like the feet of a deer and set me secure on the heights" (Ps. 18:33). The entire psalm paints a picture of David's close relationship with God, David's travails, God's fierce defense all in brilliant brush strokes. There is no mention of David's fears, his despondency or his anger. The psalm is a fine tribute to the king taking the throne, but we miss the personal touch that makes so many of the psalms so special.

The 'Song of the Bow', found in 2nd Samuel Chapter 1, is not the same. It must have been written at about the same time, but the tone is entirely different. Saul had spent well over a decade pursuing David to kill him, but David is unable to hate Saul. Instead, he laments his death: "Your glory, O Israel, is slain on your high places! How the mighty have fallen" (2nd Sam. 1:19)! He pronounces a curse over mountains of Gilboa: "You mountains of Gilboa, let there be no dew or rain upon you, nor fields of offerings" (2nd Sam. 1:21)! According to Derek Prince, the Israeli government has had a successful tree planting program throughout Israel, except on Mount Gilboa. For some unexplainable reason the trees won't prosper there. "Saul and Jonathan, beloved and lovely! In life and in death they were not divided; they were swifter than eagles; they were stronger than lions" (2nd Sam. 1:23). David, unlike Saul, has no fear or jealousy about extolling the greatness of those around him, or those who proceeded him. He perfectly shared honor where honor was due.

Discussion Points:

1. How do we see David embracing his anointing, even when kingship seemed far away?

2. Thinking of the advice around David in the wilderness, how does he keep on the right track?

3. How does David's attitude inspire greatness?

4. Saul failed in many ways. Why does David honor him as God's anointed?

5. What about David's personality might inspire you to greatness?

Application:

1. David was placed on a very clear path of providence. For many years, however, that path seemed like an impossible dream. And yet, David continued to act in a way appropriate to his destiny, until the day his destiny began to fall into place. Do you feel that you have a destiny? Is it near or far? What do you do when it is still far off?

2. We know that David had a lot of bad advice given to him throughout his life. In many cases, he had few or no reliable sources of advice. We see that time and time again, he separated himself to get with God so he could get the right answer for the moment. How do you filter the advice you get now? Would you like to change that?

3. David was able to inspire men to do things that they didn't want to do. He was able to lead men successfully when they were angry with him and wanted to stone him. Do your attitudes inspire greatness? Is there something you can do to improve that?

4. Saul had been discarded by God, but David was still able to honor his memory for what he did do well. When someone close to you fails in many ways, are you able to see the good in them still? Are you able to speak well of the good they have done, or are doing?

About the author:

William W. Wells has taught this material to youth groups and preached it before his home church. Wells is currently retired and writing, after a career as theatrical designer and a drafter. He studied for a Masters of Religious Education during an early period in a religious cult. That occurred fifty years in the past, but, if you are interested to know more about those experiences see: *A Cult Challenge to the Church*, by the author.

The author's latest book is: *Job's White Funeral; Religion and God in the Bible's Most Confounding Book*, presenting a comprehensive look at the book of Job.

Find his books at: Amazon.com under "Wm W Wells."

Made in the USA
Coppell, TX
21 March 2024